Who is this?
This is the teacher.
The teacher is takin
into the classroom.
Good morning, boys.

Good morning.
What have you got in your bag?

I have got a new football in my bag.
Take it into the yard.

Look. Look at this football.
It is new. It is yellow.
Look at this new yellow football.
I like it. I like it. Thank you.

The boys are playing football
in the yard.
The boys like the yellow football.

Look at the football.
Where is it going?

Where is the new yellow football?
Where is it?

Look in the store-room, boys.
Is the football in the store-room?

The boys are looking
in the store-room.

Where is the new yellow football?
Is it on that chair?
Is it in that desk?
Is it under that table?

Now the teacher is looking into the store-room.

The tables are dirty.
The desks are dirty.
The chairs are dirty.
What a dirty store-room.

Take that table into the yard, boys.
Put the table in the yard, please.
Now where is the
new yellow football?

Take the chairs into the yard, boys.
Put the chairs in the yard, please.
Now where is the
new yellow football?

What is that?
Is that the small mouse?
Is he in the store-room?
Is he in that desk?

The teacher is going
into the store-room.

Look, boys. Look under that desk.
Is that the new yellow football?
Is the new yellow football
under that desk?

A boy is looking under the desk.

Yes. This is the football.
I have got it.
I have got the new yellow football.

What is that?
Is that the small mouse?
Is he in the store-room?
Is he in that desk?

The boys are putting the chairs in the store-room.
The boys are putting the table in the store-room.

The chairs are dirty.
The table is dirty.
The boys are dirty.

Now the teacher is going
into the classroom.
The boys are playing in the yard.

Where is the small mouse?
Is he in the store-room?

Is the small mouse in the desk?

Yes. Yes, he is.
Look at the small mouse.
He is in the desk.
What a good mouse.

Who is taking the football
into the classroom?
Who is wearing a yellow shirt?
Who is going into the classroom?
Who is wearing a white shirt?
Who is dirty?
Who is looking at a book?